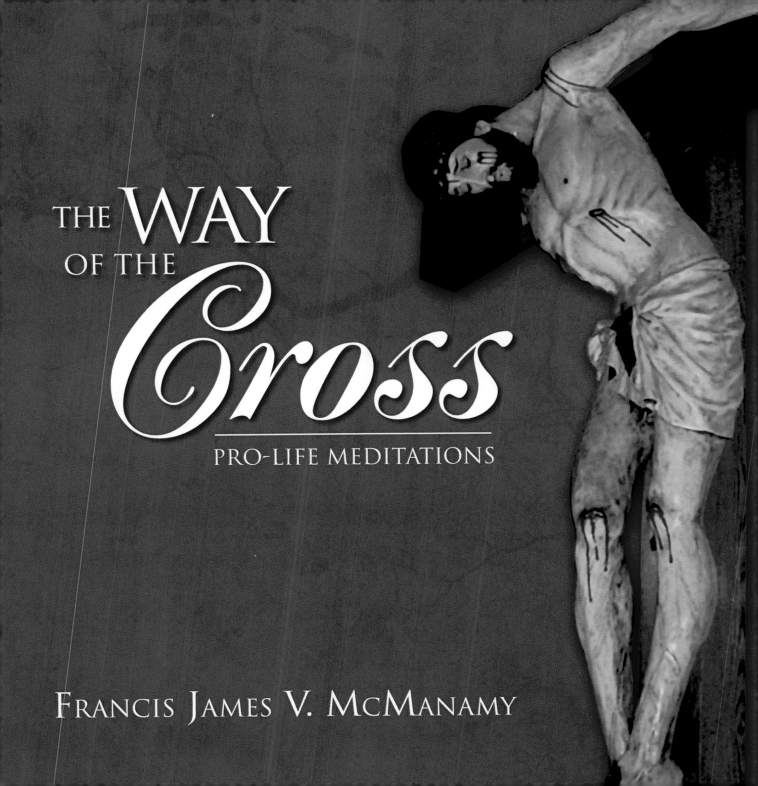

THE WAY OF THE Cross

PRO-LIFE MEDITATIONS

FRANCIS JAMES V. McMANAMY

Imprimatur

✠ Most Reverend A. F. Tonnos, D.D.
Bishop of Hamilton
December 14, 2009
Feast of St. John of the Cross

The Imprimatur is an official declaration that a book or pamphlet is free
of doctrinal or moral error. No implication is contained therein that the
granting of the Imprimatur indicates agreement with the contents,
opinions, or statements expressed.

To order additional copies of this book, contact:
Xlibris
844-714-8691
www.Xlibris.com
Orders@Xlibris.com

ISBN: Softcover   978-1-4500-2445-7
Hardcover   978-1-4500-2446-4
EBook   978-1-6698-0233-4

Library of Congress Control Number: 2010900245

Print information available on the last page

Rev. date: 12/01/2021

The Way of the Cross: Pro-Life Meditations

In loving memory of
the Servant of God, Pope John Paul II,
who boldly promoted the Culture of Life
and the Civilization of Love,

and for all mothers and fathers
who heroically persevere
in giving and sustaining human life.

. . . I have set before you life and death, blessing and curse;
therefore choose life, that you and your descendants may live,
loving the Lord your God, obeying his voice,
and cleaving to him...

Deuteronomy 30:19-20

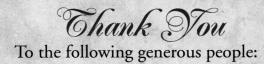

Thank You

To the following generous people:

The Most Reverend Charles Chaput, O.F.M. Cap, Fr. Marco Testa and Fr. Charles Anang, for their excellent input. You made it all possible.

Mr. Jim Hughes for his encouragement and constant support. Jim, your faith and wisdom is always the spark that gets everything going.

Mr. Jeff Gunnarson for coming on board. Jeff (alias chief), your many insights and your great sense of humour kept me going.

Mr. Dan DiRocco for giving of his time to copyedit the text. Dan, your full time apostolate in the pro-life movement since your retirement as a high school principal has been fantastic, and I feel fortunate to be one of the beneficiaries.

Miss Mary Nicol for her proofreading. Mary, your experience was invaluable.

The talented teens and young adults who produced the illustrations. Your faith shines through your inspiring work!

My colleagues at Assumption High School, Burlington, Ontario — teacher Mrs. Jody Fuller who inspired the student artists throughout the process, chaplaincy leader Mr. Lorenzo Campanelli for his friendship and support, and principal Mr. Michael Iannetta for graciously giving his permission.

Above all, this work would have been impossible without the inspiration and help of glorious Mary ever-Virgin, the mother of the Son of God, and our mother. Her discipleship in complete fidelity to the will of God inspires me to the supernatural virtue of Hope in believing that one day all human life will be respected and protected from the womb to the tomb.

Foreword

From time to time we've all heard people utter the words "all we can do is pray," which begs the question, do we consider prayer only as a last resort?

Prayer is the most powerful thing anyone can offer in any given situation, but sometimes we forget that it's the first thing we should do. The late great Canadian Pro-Life activist Joseph P. Borowski would often say "Pray to God, and <u>then</u> row for shore."

In other words, by putting those intentions, which are closest to our hearts, into the hands of God first and then doing whatever we are able, we've gotten our priorities straight.

The Holy Season of Lent offers great opportunities to once again focus on the real meaning of life and the love story of Almighty God sending us His only begotten Son, who would redeem us by His Passion, death on the Cross and His Resurrection.

These Stations of the Cross, with a particular pro-life focus, provide a poignant reminder to all of us sinners, of the need to take up daily our own slivers of His Cross, with joy and thanksgiving.

January 1st, 2010
Jim Hughes
National President
Campaign Life Coalition

Opening Prayer

Heavenly Father, Creator of the Universe, You sent Your only begotten Son to save the human race by the triumph of His suffering on the Cross, and His glorious Resurrection. As we trace these fourteen steps of His Passion, grant us the grace to work steadily for a deeper appreciation in society of the value of each human life, made in Your image and likeness. Grant this through Christ our Lord. Amen.

I

Jesus is Condemned to Death

(John 3:16; Isaiah 53:7; John 18:33, 19:1-16)

Theme: Abortion, euthanasia, human rights violations as social evils.

L. We adore You, O Christ, and we praise You.
R. Because by Your Holy Cross, You have redeemed the world.

Meditation: The destruction of innocent human life has dire social and moral consequences. *The Gospel of Life* reminds us, "[whatever] is opposed to life itself, such as any type of murder, genocide, abortion, euthanasia, or willful self-destruction, whatever violates the integrity of the human person . . . all these things . . . are infamies indeed. They poison human society. And they do more harm to those who practice them than to those who suffer from the injury. Moreover, they are a supreme dishonour to the Creator." (EV 3) Abortion is such a grave violation of the moral law that Vatican II described it as an "unspeakable crime." (GS 51) Mother Teresa of Calcutta pointed out the corruption of selfish human thinking when she declared "it is a poverty to decide that a child must die so that you may live as you wish."

Prayer: Lord of the living, we acknowledge the millions of babies who have died worldwide, many for reasons of social convenience. We pray that You will convert hearts and minds to support and protect human life from conception to natural death. Amen.

The Second Station

Jesus Takes Up His Cross

(Isaiah 53:4-6; Matthew 27:31; Luke 9:23)
Theme: The courage to be pro-life.

L. We adore You, O Christ, and we praise You.
R. Because by Your Holy Cross, You have redeemed the world.

Meditation: Jesus willingly took up His Cross after a time of temptation in the garden, where He dealt with the human reality of fear. Pregnancy is beautiful. At times however, it can be a frightening experience for many reasons: a girl is pregnant and not married; a man has lost his job and doubts whether he and his spouse can care for another child; a child has been conceived with a mental or physical deformity and the doctors are recommending abortion.

Prayer: Courageous Lord, because of human sin which instills in people a lack of faith, hope and love, we are often faced with crosses that seem almost impossible to carry. It is precisely then that You help us to carry them. Give us the courage to carry our daily cross, especially by choosing life, when those filled with the spirit of the world would rather we choose death. Amen.

III

Jesus Falls the First Time

(Isaiah 53:6)

Theme: Women and men who regret their participation in abortion.

L. We adore You, O Christ, and we praise You.
R. Because by Your Holy Cross, You have redeemed the world.

Meditation: One man writes about his experience of the loss of his child through abortion. "It was a toxic mixture of despair, regret, anger, helplessness, powerlessness, and an overwhelming feeling that something utterly tragic was about to happen . . . I felt the impact of the loss with the force of an asteroid slamming into the Earth." (Canada *Silent No More* testimony) Similarly, an Alberta woman says "Abortion killed my children, and has deeply hurt and damaged me also. We hope that young women hearing our stories will now know that abortion is not a 'safe' procedure and that it took the lives of our children." (Canada *Silent No More* testimony) Abortion hurts women, men, children, and society.

Prayer: Exhausted Lord, You were beaten, in pain, and suffering greatly, which resulted in Your first fall. Women and men have also fallen for the lies of the pro-death culture by participating in the evil of abortion. Some continue to rationalize, but many more realize the error of their ways and now seek forgiveness and healing. Bring them to the knowledge of Your eternal love and welcome them back to You. May their experience help others to avoid the scourge of abortion. Amen.

IV

The Fourth Station

Jesus Meets His Afflicted Mother

(John 19:25-27, 16-22)

Theme: Women who need healing because they are victimized by abortion.

L. We adore You, O Christ, and we praise You.
R. Because by Your Holy Cross, You have redeemed the world.

Meditation: Jesus suffered greatly seeing His mother so afflicted by His Passion. Mothers are often pressured to choose abortion, and suffer greatly afterward: their initial sense of relief soon turns to a battery of physical, psychological and spiritual problems such as guilt, anger, depression, suicidal tendencies and the inability to conceive again. There are many pro-life organizations that offer post-abortive healing, forgiveness and restoration, such as, *Second Chance Ministry*.

Prayer: Compassionate Lord, women often feel abandoned after abortion, having no peace of mind, body or soul. Surround them with the knowledge of Your tender embrace and mercy. We pray that You continue to assist organizations in our world that help women to know Your care and abiding love for them through healing and forgiveness. Amen.

V

The Fifth Station

Simon of Cyrene Helps Jesus Carry His Cross

(Matthew 27:30-32, 25:40; Galatians 6:2)

Theme: Obstacles to being pro-life.

L. We adore You, O Christ, and we praise You.
R. Because by Your Holy Cross, You have redeemed the world.

Meditation: A passerby, Simon of Cyrene, was conscripted by the Roman Soldiers to assist Jesus Christ in carrying His Cross. Jesus, exhausted and worn out by the journey, willingly received help. Pro-lifers dedicate their lives assisting others to understand that the unborn child is human and deserves full status as a person, with legal protection. We already have many historical examples of certain classes of human beings not being acknowledged as persons: African Americans, Jews, and women too. Society needs to challenge ignorance, liberal media bias, secular humanism and materialism, apathy, poverty, breakdown of the traditional family, and lack of genuine spiritual and political leadership. In doing so, like Simon, we break the cycle of evil, coldness and indifference, while making room for the warmth of God's love.

Prayer: Determined Lord, give all people of good will the wisdom and courage to believe that all human life is sacred, having been made in the image and likeness of God. May this conviction lead to the granting of full legal protection to all human beings, especially the unborn and the most vulnerable. Amen.

THE SIXTH STATION

Veronica Wipes the Face of Jesus

(Isaiah 52:14, 14:9)
Theme: Pro-life and the media.

L. We adore You, O Christ, and we praise You.
R. Because by Your Holy Cross, You have redeemed the world.

Meditation: Each person has a right to receive accurate reports of local, national and international news from the mass media. *The Gospel of Life* states "[an] important and serious responsibility belongs to those involved in the mass media, who are called to ensure that the messages which they so effectively transmit will support the culture of life . . . With great respect they should also present the positive values of sexuality and human love, and not insist on what defiles and cheapens human dignity . . . With scrupulous concern for factual truth, they are called to combine freedom of information with respect for every person and a profound sense of humanity." (EV 98)

Prayer: Suffering Lord, Veronica's deed of great charity was evident when she wiped clean Your bruised and bloodied face. We pray that members of the media, who have a great responsibility always to seek the truth in their journalism, will have the courage to defend human dignity especially since abortion, euthanasia, and immoral technologies threaten the moral fabric of society. Amen.

VII

THE SEVENTH STATION

Jesus Falls the Second Time

(Hebrews 4:15)

Theme: Political, civic and religious leaders.

L. We adore You, O Christ, and we praise You.
R. Because by Your Holy Cross, You have redeemed the world.

Meditation: The National Director of Priests for Life, Father Frank Pavone, reflects on ways in which pro-life voting can effectively end abortion. He says, "I'm motivated to vote, not because one election will end abortion, and certainly not because I expect our elected officials to be perfect or to do my work for me. The People of God have to do the work of ending abortion — providing alternatives, educating minds, changing hearts, changing laws. But part of that work is electing the people who will pose the least obstacle to that mission. We don't elect people to do our work for us, but rather people who will let us do our own work" . . . (Priests for Life Educational Resources).

Prayer: By the grace of Your second fall, O Lord, we pray for brave civic, political and religious leaders who are willing to stand for justice and protect all human beings, especially the most vulnerable. Touch them in a special way with the gift of courage — that they may withstand the forces of the culture of death, and instead promote a true culture of life. Amen.

THE EIGHTH STATION

Jesus Consoles the Holy Women of Jerusalem

(Luke 23:27-31; John 15:6)

Theme: Doctors, nurses, and those who assist in the abortion industry.

L. We adore You, O Christ, and we praise You.
R. Because by Your Holy Cross, You have redeemed the world.

Meditation: Were it not for the cooperation of people and organizations that support it, abortion could never be in our midst. We are reminded that "[doctors] and nurses are . . . responsible, when they place at the service of death skills which were acquired for promoting life. But responsibility likewise falls on the legislators who have promoted and approved abortion laws . . . on the administrators of health care centres where abortions are performed . . . [on] those who have encouraged the spread of an attitude of sexual permissiveness and a lack of esteem for motherhood, and with those who should have ensured – but did not – effective family and social policies in support of families, especially larger families and those with particular financial and educational needs. Finally, one cannot overlook the network of complicity which reaches out to include international institutions, foundations and associations which systematically campaign for the legalization and spread of abortion in the world." (EV 59) Some in our world perversely call abortion a "right." Righteous persons can never accept killing as an answer to the world's social problems.

Prayer: Understanding Lord, You consoled the holy women of Jerusalem, asking them to pray not for You, but for themselves and their children. Console us too, and give us strength in the life-giving work of salvation that comes from You. Amen.

IX

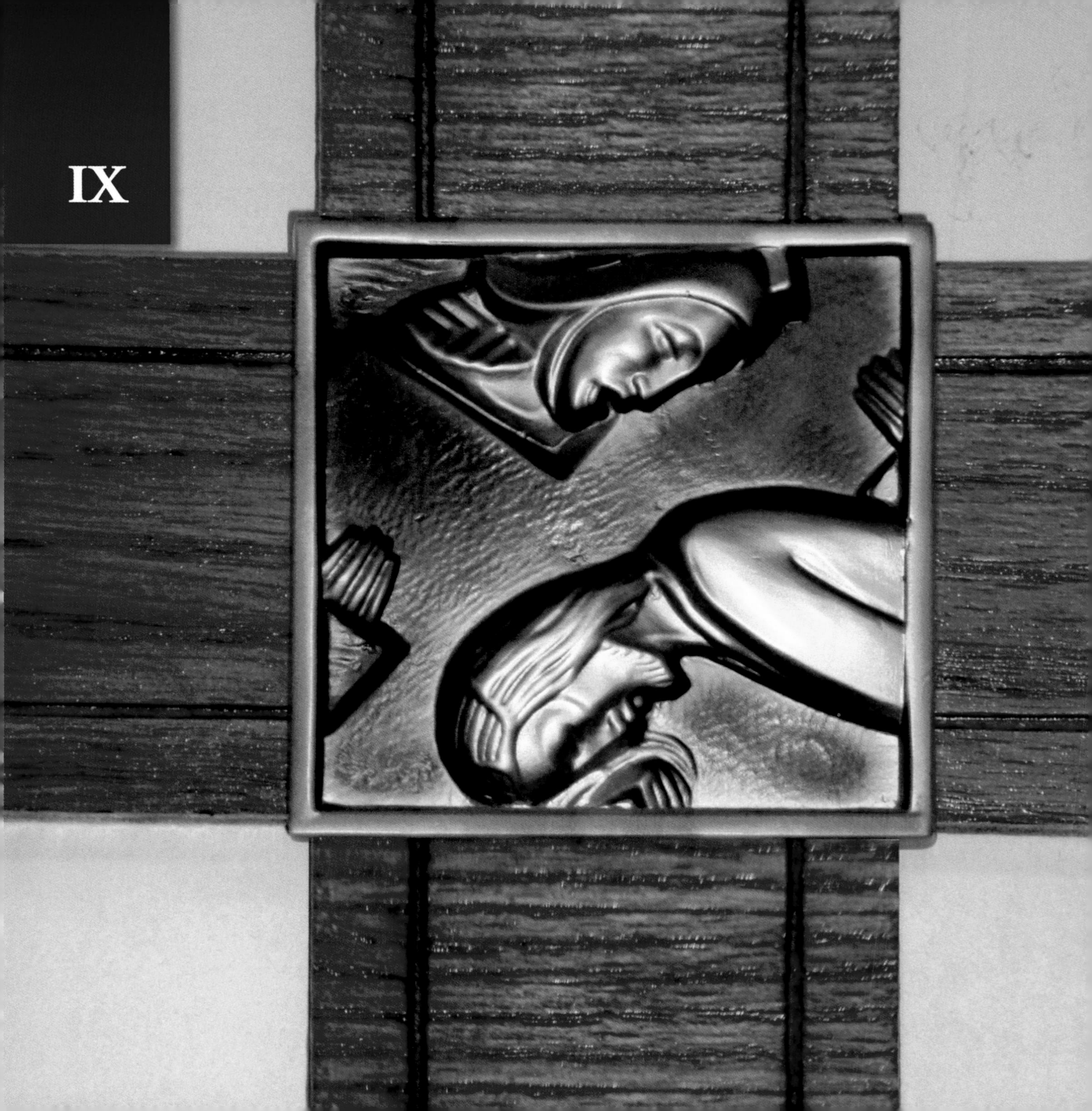

THE NINTH STATION

Jesus Falls the Third Time

(Philippians 2:5-7; Luke 14:11)

Theme: Citizenship and pro-life voters' responsibility.

L. We adore You, O Christ, and we praise You.
R. Because by Your Holy Cross, You have redeemed the world.

Meditation: In the *Voter's Guide for Serious Catholics*, Priests for Life encourages voters to cast their vote according to Christian objective moral norms, avoiding candidates who support intrinsically evil policies, especially those who support abortion, euthanasia, embryonic stem-cell research, human cloning and attacks on true marriage and the family. In this way objective moral standards are promoted, and the common good upheld.

Prayer: Faithful Lord, by the merits you won for us in Your third fall, we ask You to provide consistent leadership that will properly inform the conscience of citizens, so that voters will engage the political process with integrity, truth and justice, and that their vote will reflect principles that uphold the sanctity and dignity of human life. Amen.

X

THE TENTH STATION

Jesus is Stripped of His Garments

(John 19:23-25; Luke 13:33)

Theme: Those who work in the pro-life movement, especially
the persecuted and falsely accused.

L. We adore you, O Christ, and we praise You.
R. Because by Your Holy Cross, You have redeemed the world.

Meditation: Jesus chose to suffer for the human race. He chose to be stripped of everything, even the seamless garment that His mother made for Him. The pro-life movement has produced great heroes such as the late Honourable Joseph P. Borowski who, in constitutionally challenging the legalization of abortion, showed definitively the humanity of unborn children. Pro-life people — leaders, activists and supporters — have in God's name made heroic sacrifices. Some, while praying and peacefully witnessing have been harassed, beaten and even jailed. Others have been unjustly burdened with financial and legal bills in witnessing to life. We would do well to remember the inspiring words of peace activist Mahatma Gandhi who said "you must be the change you wish to see in the world."

Prayer: Condemned Lord, we pray that in the face of great opposition, You will give us the grace and strength to witness to life. As many great leaders were unappreciated in their time, we too must not look for the ultimate victory here on earth but with You in the life to come. Bless all pro-life heroes who continue to build the culture of life daily in their own simple ways, and may they be the inspiration for countless others to follow. Amen.

THE ELEVENTH STATION

Jesus is Nailed to the Cross

(Psalm 22:17; Zechariah 12:10; Luke 23:33)

Theme: Experimentation on human embryos.

L. We adore You, O Christ, and we praise You.
R. Because by Your Holy Cross, You have redeemed the world.

Meditation: Jesus suffered excruciating agony while being nailed to the Cross. Despite this, He kept His human dignity as Lord and Son of God. Children also have human dignity that does not depend on their size, age or state of health. Pope John Paul II taught ". . . recent forms of intervention on human embryos which, although carried out for purposes legitimate in themselves, inevitably involve the killing of those embryos . . . the use of human embryos or fetuses as an object of experimentation constitutes a crime against their dignity as human beings who have a right to the same respect owed to a child once born, just as to every person." (EV 63)

Prayer: Lord of all Truth, we humbly ask that You rebuild the conscience of our nation and world so that from the moment of conception, tiny human beings are not made subject to illegitimate experimentation, no matter how sincere the motives of those who use them in this way. Amen.

XII

Jesus Dies on the Cross

(Luke 23:46; John 19:30; Philippians 2:8-9)

Theme: Those who are recipients of euthanasia, suicide and doctor-assisted suicide.

L. We adore You, O Christ, and we praise You.
R. Because by Your Holy Cross, You have redeemed the world.

Meditation: When the Lord died on the Cross, the hopes of many were dashed. By His glorious Resurrection, He brought life from death. Because human beings are made for eternal life, aggressive medical treatment in the face of certain death is not required. (EV 65) In many places, euthanasia or "mercy killing" which is the intentional causing of death in order to eliminate all suffering, is practiced and sometimes even approved in law. Usually the perpetrators and their helpers claim that unnecessary suffering requires the termination of the suffering individuals. Yet recent studies indicate that the victim's true motives for requesting assisted-suicide often are loneliness, a sense of isolation and utter despair. (EV 64) Like abortion, suicide and death through the practice of assisted-suicide are gravely immoral. (EV 66)

Prayer: On the Cross, O Lord, You willingly took on suffering so that You could love Your sinful children to the end. Allow the terminally ill to suffer only what is necessary for their salvation. Please assist all those in the apostolic work of palliative care, that they may resist the temptation to end prematurely the life of the care-recipient, and instead provide compassionate care by easing their pain and thereby preserving each one's human dignity until natural death. Amen.

Jesus is Taken Down from the Cross

(Luke 23:50-53; John 19:31-37; Luke 24:26)

Theme: Human life comes from God and ends by His will.

L. We adore You, O Christ, and we praise You.
R. Because by Your Holy Cross, You have redeemed the world.

Meditation: Abortion ends the life of a human being within her mother's womb. Self-inflicted death and euthanasia also end the life of a human being. In these situations, someone is killed for reasons of social or financial convenience and because quality of life (both mother and child) is seen as more essential than life itself. Jesus came that each human person might have life abundantly. (John 10:10) This especially means eternal life. In the flesh, He gave His life so that each one might live. Pope John Paul II tells us "it is precisely in the "flesh" of every person that Christ continues to reveal himself and to enter into fellowship with us, so that rejection of human life, in whatever form that rejection takes, is really a rejection of Christ." (EV 104)

Prayer: Departed Lord, in the garden our first parents failed to resist the temptation to "play God." Although You had sufficiently provided for their needs, their pride led them to desire more. Give us the grace to avoid the sin of pride as we tend to the sick and suffering, and allow us to seek You with humble hearts. Help us to see our lives as a gift that comes from You alone, and returns to You in eternal life. Amen.

XIV

THE FOURTEENTH STATION

Jesus is Laid in the Holy Sepulchre

(Luke 23:50-56; John 12:24-25, Romans 6:10-11)
Theme: Respecting life promotes democracy and peace.

L. We adore You, O Christ, and we praise You.
R. Because by Your Holy Cross, You have redeemed the world.

Meditation: The Church has a special concern for those who are marginalized in society, especially the unborn, the mentally and physically challenged, and the elderly. *The Gospel of Life says,* "[when] the Church declares that unconditional respect for the right to life of every innocent person — from conception to natural death — is one of the pillars on which every civil society stands, she "wants simply to promote a human State . . . which recognizes the defense of the fundamental rights of the human person, especially the weakest, as its primary duty . . . to be actively pro-life is to contribute to the renewal of society through the promotion of the common good." (EV 101)

Prayer: Sacrificial Lamb and Lord, when You entered the Tomb, many became despondent, yet Your rising to new life destroyed the power of death forever. We too, affirm the value of human life in all of its stages, a value that is based on the natural law written in the heart of every person. We pray that You remove the moral blindness that pervades society, which does not allow certain individuals the rights of personhood, especially the unborn, and those potential and real victims of euthanasia. Amen.

Conclusion

. . . And as we, the pilgrim people, the people of life and for life, make our way in confidence towards "a new heaven and a new earth" (Rev. 21:1), we look to her who is for us "a sign of sure hope and solace."

O Mary, bright dawn of the new world,
Mother of the living, to you do we entrust the cause of life.
Look down, O Mother, upon the vast numbers of babies not allowed to be born, of the poor whose lives are made difficult, of men and women who are victims of brutal violence, of the elderly and the sick killed by indifference or out of misguided mercy.

Grant that all who believe in your Son may proclaim the Gospel of life with honesty and love to the people of our time.

Obtain for them the grace to accept that Gospel as a gift ever new, the joy of celebrating it with gratitude throughout their lives and the courage to bear witness to it resolutely, in order to build, together with all people of good will, the civilization of truth and love, to the praise and glory of God, the Creator and lover of life.

(Pope John Paul II, cited in EV 105)

References

The Holy Bible, containing the Old and New Testaments. Revised Standard Catholic Edition. Scepter : Princeton, N.J.,©1946, 1966.

John Paul II, Pope. *The Gospel of Life*: Encyclical Letter *Evangelium Vitae*. Sherbrooke, QC: Mediaspaul, 1995.

Kelowna, Marlon B., and Denise Mountenay. Canada *Silent No More* Testimony, retrieved July 14, 2009. [WWW document]. URL http://www.canacal.com/canada/testimonies.cfm

Kennedy, Fr. Leonard A, C.S.B. *Lay movements XII: Post-abortion trauma. (Second Chance Ministries)*. Catholic Insight Magazine, May 1, 2002.

Pavone, Father Frank. Priests for Life Educational Resources, Why I'm Voting Pro-Life, and Motivated (2006), retrieved July 14, 2009 [WWW document]. URL http://www.priestsforlife.org/columns/columns2006/06-11-06motivated.htm

Priests for Life Political Responsibility Center, *Voter's Guide for Serious Catholics,* retrieved July 28, 2009 [WWW document]. URL http://www.priestsforlife.org/elections/voterguide.htm

Second Vatican Council, *Pastoral Constitution on the Church in the Modern World Gaudium et Spes* (GS) (1965, Dec. 7). Promulgated by His Holiness Pope Paul VI, retrieved August 4, 2009 [WWW document]. URL http://www.vatican.va/archive/hist_councils/ii_vatican_council/documents/vat-ii_cons_19651207_gaudium-et-spes_en.html

ABBREVIATIONS

EV Evangelium Vitae *(The Gospel of Life)*
GS Gaudium et Spes *(Pastoral Constitution on the Church in the Modern World)*

Illustrations

Endorsements

The author demonstrates great passion for and knowledge of the pro-life cause and scene. Like Clarence Enzler's "Everyman's Way of the Cross," which enables us to identify with the common suffering of mankind, this little work fills a need in enabling us to identify with the unborn and their plight. May it assist people to walk with the unborn in their *via dolorosa*, in their Calvary, and bring about an end to this holocaust.

Fr. Charles Anang
Professor of Systematic Theology
St. Augustine's Seminary
Scarborough, Ontario.

F.J. McManamy's "The Way of the Cross: Pro-Life Meditations," combines the Passion of Christ with the pro-life movement's efforts to educate and defend all life, from conception to natural death.

He quotes liberally from relevant literature and from famous people, including Pope John Paul II and Mother Teresa, who spoke out against the evils rampant in our culture.

There is much on which to meditate as we follow Christ on the road to Calvary.

Mary Nicol
Retired Catholic Teacher
Toronto, Ontario.

Printed in the United States
by Baker & Taylor Publisher Services